LATE STARS

Wesleyan New Poets ❖

✤ LATE STARS

Jeffrey Skinner

 **Wesleyan University Press**
Middletown, Connecticut

Some of the poems in this book appeared originally in these magazines: "On the Failure of All Love Poems," *The Atlantic*; "Ballad of the Lighthouse Keeper's Widow," *Blue Unicorn*; "Song Beginning in Summer," *The Georgia Review*; "On the Day," *The Greenfield Review*; "Knife Scars on a Plate," *Ironwood*; "August," "Possessions," *kayak*; "His Side/Her Side," *Poetry*; "Elizabeth and the Blizzard," *Poetry Northwest*; "Poppy," "Family Reunion," *Poetry Now*; "Nominal Acrostic," *Prairie Schooner*.

"His Side/Her Side" also appeared in the 1981 edition of *Anthology of Magazine Verse & Yearbook of American Poetry*.

I would like to thank the corporation of Yaddo and The Connecticut Commission on the Arts for their generous support.

Thanks also to my friends Dick Allen, Chris Millis, and Sarah Gorham for their patient help in the preparation of the manuscript.

All inquiries and permissions requests should be addressed to the Publisher, Wesleyan University Press, 110 Mt. Vernon Street, Middletown, Connecticut 06457.

Distributed by Harper & Row Publishers, Keystone Industrial Park, Scranton, Pennsylvania 18512.

Library of Congress Cataloging in Publication Data

Skinner, Jeffrey. Late stars.
I. Title. PS3569.K498L3   1984   811'.54   84-7495
ISBN 0-8195-2120-5 (alk. paper)
ISBN 0-8195-1121-8 (pbk.: alk. paper)

Manufactured in the United States of America

First Edition
Wesleyan New Poets

for my Mother and Father

for Sarah

Contents

I

Song Beginning in Summer   3

Nominal Acrostic   4

Sesshin   5

"The Incredulity of St. Thomas,"
    Gerrit Van Honthorst, c. 1617   6

Calendar of Events   8

Knife Scars on a Plate   9

Ballad of the Swimming Angel   10

Possessions   11

On the Day   13

Letter to the Muse of Bridgeport   15

Levittown, L.I., 1957   17

Spring Concert   19

August   21

II

Strange Light   25

Why She Wept   25

Looking in the Mirror at Midnight   26

The Injured Parties   26

Not Yet   27

Ad Out   27

Beginning with a Fragment of
    Thomas Merton   28

Poppy   28

Family Reunion   29

Variation on a Theme by
    Sherwood Anderson   29

Lonely Dialogue   30

In Scalzi Park   30

You, Wind   31

For Susan Dwyer   31

Corona: Against Rilke   32

III

Elizabeth and the Blizzard   39

His Side / Her Side   41

A Death Recorded as Accidental   44

Breaking Down on the New England Thruway   45

Dragonfly Dance   47

Melinda   48

Trevor and the Swarm of Gnats   49

A Dream Shared in the Country   50

Conception in Venice   52

Rolling in Clover   53

On the Failure of All Love Poems   54

Song for Prophecy in a Rainy Season   55

I

An old woman said to Shaikh Mahmah: "Teach me a prayer so that I may find contentment. So far I have always been a prey to discontent, but I now wish to be free."

The shaikh replied: "A long time ago I withdrew into a sort of fortress behind my knee to seek ardently that which you desire; but I have neither felt it nor seen it. So long as we do not accept everything in the way of love, how can we be content?"

—Attar

Song Beginning in Summer

That gentle static
of leaves in wind
is not God's breath—
He's passed on

to better things
though he has fond memories
of us. The stars
are tied

to a weavy skyline
by thin cords
of light,
like yachts

tied to the pier.
But who can
lift concrete belief
out of change?

Leaves fall,
snow stacks
neatly on the shelves
of blue spruce,

the sky hardens.
Winter circles
the harbor; abandoned
hulls crack;

less and less
we dream of summer.

Nominal Acrostic

Just barely ahead of my habits I realize
eventually they will perform final surgery.
For a long time nothing occurs to me,
for a long time I make nothing my passion.
Reality has a thin, metallic surface tension
every good boy wants to penetrate badly.
Yes, my fist is bleeding slightly, don't worry.

Sign here sign there don't smudge the paper.
Kick one habit, watch the others go wild.
In one sphere of the swimming brain
nothing is said, the air rings; in another
nothing's not wet, gills are sliced in my neck.
Eventually they will perform final surgery.
Reality has a thin, metallic surface tension.

Sesshin

The master will not listen to our problems.
He tells me to get the mountain
into my poem. I sit with the others,
dead tired, hungry. Each day we looked out
through thin air to distant strings
of wood smoke and the dark sweep
of hawk wing against blue. Banyon Lake
burns off its mist below us. We are weak,
all of us, our voices in tatters,
and the flight of any one of a million
sparrows makes light of our ambition.
Still the master does not talk. He walks
among us on this last morning like a form
of light, without sound. He claps twice,
two shots out over the valley,
and I begin to stand, thinking
I have learned little more than how to
ache at night. Suddenly he is there,
his hands inches from my face. He claps
again, and I see the stumps of two fingers
missing from his left hand and the mountain
shrinks to the size of a hat
that just fits my head, then shrinks
further into a trumpet to announce breakfast.
I blow for all I'm worth. Smell of bacon
and potatoes in mountain air, strong
coffee, all the stars chased from my eyes.

"The Incredulity of St. Thomas," Gerrit Van Honthorst, c. 1617

1

The nail of his index barely visible,
sunk deep in the wound, Thomas is all eyes
by implication—he is turned from us,
leaving Christ's torso to the light.

The body is young! I am ashamed
of my soft waist, ashamed of the time
I spent, head tilted back in the mirror, far
from compassion. A perfect center turns

beneath skin stretched taut
and delicate over the sternum, His
hands relaxed, palms out, poised to heal.
The lips are feminine, full of forgiveness

and the sweet taste of distant planets.

2

It's clear the eyes, the dark eyes of Jesus
rest on Thomas's forehead, where suddenly
there is an opening, as if he had stepped
from thick woods into a clearing

nowhere in this world. But the light
we're given falls through a stone window
and includes only the shoulders and the back
of Thomas's head; nearly the entire

body of Christ. I stand a long time
in the empty museum, looking hard, and still
something in me begs for more detail—
that part of Thomas painted over by shadow,

the doubt vanishing from my perspective. . . .

Calendar of Events

There is a blind child playing with pieces of glass in the cellar.
There is a strand of flesh still dangling from the spear's tip
      as the fire is kicked apart, and the thin smoke rises
      toward stars.
There are cars abandoned in fields that grow into nests of loneliness.
There is the nipple, and there is the mouth that wants to close
      over the nipple, and the distance between the two imperceptibly,
      eternally enlarging.
There is the eye that began in a star, the exploded iris a dazzling
      palace of hydrocarbons.
There·is an ape dipping rags in gasoline and smiling.
There is the fly that owes the spider money, can't pay, and lays
      down its quick blue life for the debt.
There is rain like gray nails, the man out walking without a coat,
      a purpose in mind, women leaning from windows and laughing,
      rainwater sputtering around his steps like liquid fire.
There is the shore I can never remember, even though I knew, I
      knew those trees and sand, that sun like my own thoughts.
There is a fish walking delicately on its spine over rocks,
      leaving a thin trail of milk.
There is a train racing its own reflection in a lake, bending
      into itself as the track darkens and the passengers fall
      asleep.
There are businessmen knocking back on-the-rocks doubles in a room
      surrounded by dark, oily wood. A waitress stands in the center
      of the room, struggling with the hooks of her brassiere.
There is a boy who drops his cotton candy into the guts of a Ferris
      wheel. He lunges, and the iron seat grows large above him.
There is an insect with tiny horns and green blood dreaming
      a kingdom of ants.
And there is the beautiful suicide, breathing at last as slowly
      as she wanted, spreading her golden hair in the earth.

Knife Scars on a Plate

The body wears down like an old plate
upon which the elements are feasting.
Faded blue flowers . . . I look up from honest work
to read the gray script wound tightly in the clouds.
No message, it says. Or, *Go back to work.*

Over my head, I imagine true love
opening like a blue spinnaker, flooding with salt air.
The journey picks up, morning light
in the kitchen takes on a Parisian roundness.
But even this is something to amuse, to occupy

until the ten thousand hooks pull out of my body
and I am painted directly onto day —
thin transparency of my smallest movements,
forgotten name, eyes that leap into the moment's center.
The long desire for cellular love,

not another sweet taste through a grid,
has led me here. Deep joy like dolphin leaping
in my chest, the borderless waters of childhood,
      rising . . .
At last the meeting is held, in a robin's skull.
The universe fits snugly. The intricate gates,

trip-switches and synapses all open
at once, the sun roars back through my eyes
and stars hurl themselves out of memory, out of breath.
Furred hands, and the moon in the cave's mouth . . .
Knife scars crossing on a white plate . . .

Ballad of the Swimming Angel

In the dusty light of an attic room he woke,
pulled on jeans and a leather jacket and went out.
He saw huge tanks rise and fall in steel cages,
saw the skyline shimmer, begin to smoke.
And saw the poor, bunched at corners, wait-
ing for the light, dreaming of higher wages.

Hello to the cop blowing into cupped hands;
a wave to each clerk inside each store,
moving quietly as fish. He turns to the ocean.
He arrives. But something about the sand's
flat color sends him flying along the shore
as the surf makes its endless corrections,

and wind stirs the bright flakes of sleep
on the water's surface. It is so still
so early, and the poor angel forbidden to swim.
But, naked, he dives between green pleats
of wave, kicks down deeper and deeper, until
he wakes in the dusty light of an attic room.

Possessions

The small bird that walks in its sleep
belongs to me. And the old man
who trips on a dirt road at dusk,
one strand of white hair blown straight
above his head like a thin flame,
he also belongs to me.
The ragged essence of green
like a heavy curtain at the forest's
edge, and the sky that disappears
as I shut my eyes: mine.
But not the clouds. The cables
I throw to them pass through
and fall to my feet;
no one owns the clouds.
The news, the bad news that arrives
in threes, and leaves in one
body is mine. And the tiny belief
I swallowed like a seed
years back: dry leaves rattle
in my lungs, branches open into hands,
roots that once ripped through
thick leather, fray: still mine.
Friends, all the lies you've inhaled,
all the snuffed prayers
for happiness whispered in my
presence belong to you—
I could do nothing with my own.
Only the dappled wren
that smashes itself against
the kitchen window, the crumpled dress,
the drop of blood on the white sill,

and the sullen one, sitting alone
in the alcove, dark master of childhood
who will no longer look me in the eye,
is mine, is mine, is mine.

On the Day

On the day inside turns out and the out-
side caves in, I'll watch your face invert
then all of you collapse. It will happen,
my friend: raw, practical organs

stitched to our walking forms. No more
mirrors. No one beautiful enough to laugh.
Then sky may continue to open
and close, shutter an exact measure of light,

but blue will be green, green blue,
and red yellow. On that day a triangular sun
will set with a sigh in the north,
rivers flow sideways, clouds move up

and down like plump submarines, lovers
bathe in sky and sail home on a tidy wave
of ingrown lawn; all before the difference
can be explained. This is the landscape

once safe under layers of sleep,
spoken of in dim rooms in hushed voices
as the dead are prepared for their gardening.
But you and I, my friend, on the day

inside turns out and outside in,
we'll go on as usual: barbecues on concrete
patios, snow falling to the grill,
Christmas in July, cold sweat in October,

the delicate pain of contact.
And we'll keep praying that at least one
angel might return out of tenderness or frenzy
and change us, wrench vision outward,

give back the body of childhood
glittering with stars and the good blue eyes
pointed toward death even then
as if it were the right direction.

Letter to the Muse
of Bridgeport

There are tiny holes in the music
corresponding to the shadows leaves cast
on themselves. I watch the wind shuffle
these shadows and the maples
appear to shiver. I write to tell you
I am not happy or unhappy in this season
uncurling over the fresh lawns
of Fairfield. I have given that up.
Now I focus all doubt on the sky
with its concrete clouds, and the spongy
firmness of treeline in middle
distance. And I write only to report
the senses loosen as the light inside
the rubber plant leaf, for example,
gains intensity, and the brown
ceramic pot gleams on the porch floor,
still and perfect in a rectangle of sun.
You seem so close as I write you—
can you hear the gulls complain
from their spirals over river garbage?
I have never lived far from that city
we discovered out of love. In fact
you can see the buses from there
dragging their black clouds through
this town, and ageless kids from Sylvan
Beach tracking sand through the booze
and record stores I now live near.
We were always talking, remember,

about love and its divisions
as we lay on that beach. I remember
the oil burning on your body, your sea
smell as we made love later. Now
if you come to me you will find weight
and doubt layered on, change nothing—
the old desire for love has grown
precise, urgent, radiant with clarity.
Come. Every so often a blue tile
breaks loose from the sky and falls
into my hands. The music of past and future
flows through the tiny holes of leaf shadow.
The tree sways firmly in the present.

Levittown, L.I., 1957

At seven, I tried to poke a hole in my shadow,
my sword and its raised in unison
on mother's clean sheet. I succeeded
and got hell for it. Next door
Dave Brown believed in walking naked

in front of his children. The block
buzzed—even I knew he hated his job.
Leaning back against the refrigerator
he'd sing ("Just like Perry Como!")

while we kids swarmed on the linoleum floor,
red lights flashing from our Sputnik caps,
mad for our transistors. I hammered
an old clock apart in the attic
but kept the pieces, my first lesson

in creation. And every night out at dusk
for stickball in the narrow street—
Danny could nail every pitch,
send it to old man Cummings's front step

for a home run and a lost ball.
When the lamps came on we'd sift away
toward our mothers' voices.
Levittown—planned honeysuckle,
communal pools, carports, Good Humor!

(No one wants to sing your flat yards
and young hopeful parents, the fathers
drinking at home, the mothers'
eyes shining like polished sinks. . . .)

Walking to Laurel Elementary
in the rain, the smell of coffee
drifting from the widow's house, the future
unimaginable, distant as next week;
flannel shirt sticking to my smooth chest.

Spring Concert

1

Wasps hover over the eaves of the old
administration building. Slow clouds
steam by, ironing out the horizon.

While the band tunes up in the gym
we have a little time to relax. Come,
sit with me in the triangular shade,

the black prism beneath the grand-
stand. So much glass, yes, so many
twisted rings and empty cans

glitter here, but they are only
last season's enthusiasm, they've lost
their bite. . . . Did you, or I, or was it

we who went to this school?
To me it was all humiliation and lust.

2

Popular songs in march time
form a pattern on the green diamond.
I can't make it out, my attention's

drawn to the redhead on tuba—
ballooning cheeks, eyes squeezed
behind thick glasses, white-knuckled

determination either
to play clean or simply not drop
the damn thing. So beautiful, pressed

uniforms, clumsy music, green under blue,
wasps, clouds . . . although I think
the clouds are too fat, I think spring

has never hurt them, I think they
should be clipped and pasted in the Yearbook.

3

Speeches, batons, daffodils in the Queen's
arms. More songs. Would you listen
for me . . . I squirm in the folding

chair, look down at my
feet resting in two pools of grass
and the ant working there, pincers locked

in the emerald head of a Japanese
beetle. Over rough terrain,
though beetle struggles, ant

makes steady progress. Applause. You pull
me up by an arm. Sun leaches a shine
from the bald heads of fathers, the Principal

shakes the Bandmaster's hand.
The field breaks into bright young faces.

August

All summer the boats grew smaller,
late stars popped or quietly
withdrew. Often our talk
stalled and we would turn
our hands over and stare at them,
thinking vaguely about time
and its ripped silks
fluttering in the background.
We made a vow to awaken,
broke it, made it again.
Evenings, in the soft crack
between light and dark
we saw ourselves floating
east, heading out to sea as mist
and had to pull back, hard.
Sailing there once
I was caught through inattention
by the hollow metal boom
and swept off. It took
the dead weight of my body
to lift me from the thick
cold water and right the mast.
Back on shore, women
tried to tell the future
written in the ribs of sand,
but soon lost faith
in their method. Then it wasn't
long before someone
noticed the trees throw
a few tentative leaves
to the ground, the sun

drift off. And we stopped
looking for signs in the waves
or sky for whatever difference
we make. The sand was cold
and spiked with thin
shadows of grass as I walked
back to my car,
a dozen small shells clicking
together like moons
in the wet pocket of my jeans.

II

There is a woman with whom we never attain complete
sincerity, even though we know that she knows us
inside out and that we, ourselves, may count on her
benevolence.

—Remy de Gourmont

Strange Light

The dendrites in our bodies need sun.
We feel them leaning like little trees.
A bruise, apple-shaped, appears on her skin.
Strands of her hair tremble in the breeze.
All I ever wanted was all, all of it—
Did you think I arrived with nothing?
Sam leaps in the air for his stick,
Margie dials the wrong number, not thinking.
The roads are bad, stay with me tonight.
We'll pretend there's a fire and stare
at each other for warmth. Afraid but open
is how we feel about this strange light
clinging to our edges now as we turn
to another life, clouds in the upper air.

Why She Wept

She explained why she wept in her sleep.
He kissed her, got up to look for the time.
Half-past, everyone. She wanted to keep
his faults, not argue his love of wine;
she wanted to limit her pain to the present,
not feel it settle over all her life. . . .
He, a writer, should understand resentment,
the little cries when he'd whisper *wife.*
"O but sometimes the line comes easy,
a sudden gust of wind lifts the curtain
and the angel is quietly with me in the room.
Sometimes the nerves are too busy—
my hand wavers over the paper, sprung loom
trying to dream back the first pattern."

Looking in the Mirror at Midnight

Stoned out and tired after a bad movie,
the girl gone. Dishes huddle in the sink.
Metallic red-and-white cans of Coke,
cheap towers on the books piled before me—
no single object I own says *sad*, or *happy*.
I am bent enough to ask wind to speak,
then I am amazed by the way I take
wind for granted, its sheets and pulleys
yanked tight in the trees and the earth
sailing. Before that serious woman came,
stupid with the joy of partial knowledge
I walked here, feet cut by the edge
of the present. One push more and the lame
man facing me may hurry out of birth.

The Injured Parties

Whatever this enormous life wants to say
I seem to be stuck across the room
trying to read lips. Oh, unhappy
girl, crying among coats in the bedroom,
it was your idea!—this party, this heart
trying to weave two hallways inside.
There are many of us standing apart—
the rounded, the lethal place to hide.
What they told us to do we have done;
for ourselves we lie and make love
on separate sheets, married to the phone.
Once, I showed you a worn rock I kept
from childhood. You said *breath won't move
out of a past so clean, so well swept.*

Not Yet

The tired collection of ghost kisses,
the hips and thighs that move and blur
churning, as the skin reminisces,
dark eye covered by clef of dark hair—
the old way of going back is dead.
I left her to watch river gulls
draw slow curves in blue, unafraid
of the oily water, the rocks below.
One gull breaks off from the others
and dips down to see if I'm
edible, or a piece of moving meat,
not yet interesting. That's what I am.
I spit once in the blackened river,
turn and walk home on my own two feet.

Ad Out

Flung two hundred pounds against the wall,
rolled off, slid to the floor, aching.
Two perfect blue eyes that missed the ball
squeeze tight. Look, look: a big man crying.
Whereas once he was godlike master
of the straight-arm and the leap
through nests of arms and plastic armor
now the body moves as if half-asleep—
body that gave pleasure has given notice.
But what replaces the sensual life,
where is the window to make an exchange?
He doesn't know. Coming to his senses,
he leaves the court, drives home to the wife
and the long emptying into middle age.

Beginning with a Fragment
of Thomas Merton

A pure love, disinterested and free,
each passion given only its exact time,
skin cold or neutral to the touch of money;
how lonely, how far away from what I am!
An embarrassment, to give you flowers
I have stolen, and must someday pay for.
But we'll feel better in a few hours,
when the drug wears off. I'll lock the door,
watch the blurred room snap into focus. . . .
O hold me against various dreams of perfection,
your mouth small and guiltless on my cheek
your smooth body one long, impure caress!
(Let's just kill him, that angel who sneaks
up and begs, as if we were more than human.)

Poppy

The great machine winds down, your finger-
tips turn blue, the sluiced urine drips out.
Glasses on, bent frames; my face is a warm blur.
And all but the distant past is in doubt. . . .
I hold your hand, lightly, so as not
to add another rose or plum-colored bruise
to the garland climbing your arm. Your weight:
seventy-six pounds. Almost nothing left to lose.
O flesh and bone, thin as a wire sculpture
lifted in and out of bed, chair, bath,
wheeled to the day room from two to four
by Jamaican nurses with their easy laugh—
listen to this voice rising from my childhood,
There, there, you loved me. Feel this hand.

Family Reunion

The scream is cut from a block of ice.
No big deal, please. Put it on the back seat,
but use the tarp. Uncle Red took a slice
and sat away from us; the dim heat
of his lunacy moved me at the picnic.
No one there knew Thomas Merton,
though we said grace, and some were Catholic.
But sure as God they knew their burden,
each his own: cancerous jaw, schizophrenia,
and those isolate perfect ones who hated
their one life, the same trees each morning.
My inheritance—a seed, a crystal aphasia
planted in me at seven, still growing,
blocking the scream and the frozen blood.

Variation on a Theme by
Sherwood Anderson

How can I be holy when the garbage stinks,
and I can only take it out on certain days?
Come closer, Who believes the sky thinks?
Childhood in a velvet case, yes, a gold haze
dead center I carry everywhere, delicately,
as if it were an egg nothing touched. But
who dreams of being holy in this city?
—Three million windows opaque with dust;
the watery sound of money changing hands
pours through the cracks of our apartments.
And the woman upstairs refuses to turn down
her terrible music. And the many nights
now I walk out, stand on the black lawn
throwing kisses the black sky understands.

Lonely Dialogue

Seagulls overhead sign the river unholy
across blank sky. But this is a figure,
you object, an imputation of anomie
when in fact they scavenge with order,
they pick the bank clean out of love.
True . . . *Seagulls overhead sign the river
unholy.* Under the frozen crust water moves,
gulls fly above, the moon will rise after
everyone living this moment is dead—
Why are you so damn illusive and sad?
No. Please, the seagulls overhead sign
the river unholy. I say nothing more.
It must be cold flying in the sun's stare,
   you concede,
it's cold here. But not by the river's design.

In Scalzi Park

I saw the shadings of faint green
brushed here and there across park grass
still a wiry brown in most places;
some hope had placed me in the scene.
There was the dark smell of wet trees,
and dogs fighting on the riverbank.
But where was he, whom I wanted to thank,
even his absence? Then that release . . .
Rain, fall back, tell him I'm past
caring how trees sleep through phases;
spring moon overhead, rich and obscene.
I saw the shadings of faint green
brushed here and there across park grass
still a wiry brown, beaten into place.

You, Wind

You, leaf-swallower, wind, talk to me.
Play with my hair like a mother.
Tell me again how my old life was happy.
The tented sky of New England is smaller
in winter. The cat refuses to go out.
A partial list of renunciations: booze,
the sad targets of lust, books, shout-
ing silently for all the good it all does.
I thought maybe if I walked away
from the house, to the unthinking stream,
if I could see thin lines of snow
melt on the splayed branches of willow
and drop soundlessly as snow in a dream,
then; but the wind asks no one to stay.

For Susan Dwyer

It's all at once the heart wants to open.
Late stars lean down to singe my hair,
early morning. I never really let you in—
but then, you knew that. Remember noon air
we'd breathe at the edge of Bridgeport,
perched on the sea wall, rapt, talking poetry,
snapping line by line through "Alien Report"?
It didn't occur to us we were happy. . . .
Now we live ten miles apart and never speak.
Your thin husband has gone, and *she*,
she has not abandoned, I think, but left me
for some little quiet that will not break.
Susan, I look at morning stars and I burn
for that decade I spent, arrogant and alone.

Corona: Against Rilke

1

If I were made better I'd like it more.
Chasing over the surface of an iron song,
the feeling of "having been here before"
decides too many arguments. This tongue
perched on a shaky twig may burst
into flame or the form of a sparrow
any minute now. And, you say, it's only the first
body part to leave through the window—
the rest will follow. But who will witness
my body's abandonment? Does the wind
have strength enough to carry me,
feather by feather, toward a finer assembly?
I've had enough of those advocates of bliss
who live on air. I'll fly down instead.

2

Who lives on air? I'll fly down instead,
breathing pleasure through ciliate brain
cells, dancing all night for the dead
who are never bored. A little refrain:
what light, what lust, what light . . .
repeat until the authorities arrive.
We've been waiting for unaccountable nights,
in fact, in a warm little hopeless dive
where an illuminated clock turns slowly
over the bar, and shots are dirt cheap.
There's a girl there who'll count to five
as you slip each finger in. Neon heat.
No one harping on and on about how to survive.
Everything hidden, as it should be.

3

Everything hidden as it should be,
including the cups and saucers, the chipped
statues, the house pets and the shrouded trees.
Some of the angels, we suspect, abdicated,
Rilke—those left have let themselves go.
And not one of us has the heart for winter—
we won't permit the cracked red skin to show.
The guests hang on, hang on after dinner.
Then at work sometimes the old rage
comes back, and I have to reach
for a pencil and let the simple love
of numbers align me. Hard to prove
grief against money: takes years of research.
I pour through page after page after page.

4

I pour through page after page after page,
paper-cut, ink stains on my lips and teeth,
sad whoosh of tires in the street
floating to my window. I close your book. These days
are not yours: no castles, no polished bays
to glide clouds, no sigh of a cliff
windstruck and severe. Nothing you'd call a cliff.
Light rushes like water through these days.
But the nights, Rilke, the nights are still
like the panther you studied
into hard lines: fluid, wound tight as hell,
padding over the city, yellow-eyed.
That is something we can believe,
the careful stalk, the bared, all-out heave.

5

The careful stalk, the bared, all-out heave
of feathery back-lit spore into thin air.
Those light crystals we had to leave
in childhood begin to matter
more now, now they become something
to destroy. For example: take any green
lawn, a slightly red-faced man mowing,
a woman inside gently shifting corn
in boiling water, and the boy who talks
mad dreams to the sled in the attic—
can this pure, common scene be a trick
intended to lure us away from spiritual
matters? No. Yes. The boy, out for a walk,
looks guilty, as if about to whistle.

6

Looks so guilty. As if about to whistle
Scarlatti in the careful rain now falling
around him, his eyes clear, and full.
Rilke, are you still listening?
I wanted to ask about the flame
you see sometimes across
the shoulders of young women
or over the surface of a lake at dusk—
there were times, times I came that close!
The boy is me. At last, ready to give up
and let everything change
the way it wants, for a moment I stop
holding tight, and so does the rain.
Dawn opens inside the city: a brick rose.

7

Dawn opens inside the city, a brick rose.
In a small room, the student Krakkus
labors against your image. He knows
only the slightest prayer to touch Orpheus
but writes on and on, trying to climb
out of his body. He has a thousand sons.
Rilke, I have tied a scarf to each limb
of your tree! They flutter in the sun.
And when caught, I am caught
with one hand in the higher regions,
one roaming the city beneath the skin.
But it happens slow, this tearing apart
of thick fabric. Morning: the body wan, sore.
"If I were made better I'd like it more."

III

Only in others can you wash your face, it's no use to bathe it in yourself.

—Attila Jozsef

Elizabeth and the Blizzard

1

Experience has darkened what might have been
cornflower blue eyes. Cooped up three days,
she takes a dozen hard looks in the mirror
to see how delicately time has entered
her pale skin, there to transform itself
into chemicals she can't imagine, and so cares
nothing about. She wants only to get on
with bills, traffic, relatives, washing dinner
dishes (her beauty's vague, barely visible
to her); let the clouds do what they will.

2

With a sudden heave the wind slams shut
the unlatched screen door on the porch and she
starts and the cup she is washing breaks in her
hands. The cup is bone china, with red and gold
flowers, one of mother's set, the last.
She sits down at the kitchen table and cries,
silently, like a girl hiding in a neighbor's
barn in Poland, thirty-five years ago,
because she had stolen candles, and seen
what they did to women for lesser crimes.

3

On the last night of the blizzard I taunt her
once too often and she touches madness: everything
in reach goes flying: books, food, candlesticks,
meat timer, forks and knives, old betrayals. . . .
A dead shot, she tacks my hair to the wall and
demands an answer, *now*. I tell her I'm afraid
of generalities, that I need her sudden movements,
her intimate ties to the moon, her watery
pull. She is happy with this, and lets me fall
freely and with love to the kitchen floor.

4

We forgive each other, rock quietly together,
go to bed. I sleep. She stays awake, staring
through the purple window, listening to the plows
stutter and clank down the caked streets. The moon
is erratic, weakened and blocked by the storm.
If she knew what to say she would wake me,
she would wake me and tell me, then she could sleep.
But the words have hardened and camouflaged
their color in her blood, like rubies in a glass
of red wine. She watches snow fall into morning.

His Side

There can be no explanation
elaborate enough to satisfy your curiosity.
Don't you see that yet? When the hurt
has nowhere to go it becomes a kind of hunger,
a sad relish for lewd detail. And the questions
lead to nothing, like a series of doors

in a dream. Behind the next door
you keep hoping to find an explanation
but all you find is another door, a question
that opens and closes on curiosity,
so blank and wooden it hurts.
They say the best way to stop hunger

is abstention: for two days you are hungry,
then it disappears. Refrigerator doors
lose their pull, all the body's tiny hurts
heal themselves. I could explain
how the cells, freed from digestion . . . but you are not
    curious
in the least; you want to get back to the question.

She was nothing to me. You question
this, over and over, as if you hungered
for a different answer. I'm curious—
if I said it was love, wouldn't you open the door
and toss me out, screaming *Bastard*? Explanation
would be unnecessary. You would still hurt.

I'm not making fun of your hurt.
Nothing goes rancid like a promise. The question
is how many times must I explain
that what flared in me was momentary hunger,

an unexpected knock on some ancient door
I answered out of curiosity.

Like the cat, I gave in. And curious
as it sounds, though I wasn't killed I was hurt.
Yes, me! You point to the door,
you cry, you will not stop your questions—
I'm trying to tell you it was hunger
for love that brought me back. To explain

further is to mock explanation: Curious,
I indulged a brief hunger. You were hurt.
Our love is not in question. Now, shut the door.

Her Side

It's like you to fall back on words
when what I need is the touch
of something real. Oh, how calmly you say the damage
is done, that I should forget her,
forget my sad, my pointless questions
so that we can go on living—

what a fairy tale you must live
in! To think I'd swallow smooth words
and idiotic, cliché reasons without question—
the height of arrogance! Touch
down from your cloud, friend. Describe her
face, her body: let the damages

take on flesh. Was she ever damaged
like me? Or did she have a life
you read about in *Cosmopolitan,* her
clothes sleek and shiny, good with words,
up-to-date on every kind of touch
to bring a man off? Does that question

offend you? Ha! What a question!
Tell me, did you satisfy her? Or would it damage
your pride to answer? It's touching,
your concern about our life
together, how it hurt to break your word,
how you wavered in agony. But what about her,

we have to consider her
feelings too, don't we? Now you question
my sincerity, call me sarcastic. Words
cannot express how sorry I am. It's damaging
evidence, I know, my disregard for her life. . . .
You see, the thing is, I've lost my touch

for empathy. All I see is your hand, touching
her there, and there, lifting her
out of some hell, and into my life.
Why? why?—that's the only question
I want answered. Why did you damage
a promise I thought went beyond words,

and now is just words? You can't touch
me now without damage: I think of her.
Answer the question, bastard. Don't waste my life.

A Death Recorded as Accidental

Against the pull of train whistles,
cool, sweet blue cries, there is the pull
of bad years. Sitting on his screened-in
porch, sampling the breezes of September,
a man misses his wife for the first time
in years. No revelation perfumes the wind,
he is only mildly surprised. He gives in
to the pull and thinks for a decent wage
the sky might break down to reliable
gradation—the hunting trip replanned
for a day the sun was scheduled
to be open, and relaxed. But no one
has that kind of money. The sky darkens
whenever it feels the urge. The man is surprised
because he knows his wife comes back
each season of her death: winter, her smile
all done by wires, earrings like tiny
chandeliers nestled in her dark hair,
the lines of her body covered by miles
of white fur, she comes back,
and the hot ice of her eyes burns away
all his desire. . . . Another train
goes by; he stares through the smoky whiskey
in his hand, feels the pull surround
his heart. What simple things he wanted
to say!—left in bars and airports,
hidden in the deep crease between car seats
or frozen in the long whistle of a train
he should never have missed. That year
he called all her pleas delusion,
he came upon the body and the blood
flung over snow. And he could only sit there
and smoke, the still-life before him
impossible to leave, or carry home.

Breaking Down on the
New England Thruway

The wheel vibrates, tries to shake off
my hands; the car leans like a wounded fish
as I struggle to land it on the shoulder.

The trunk is surprising: a pair
of women's tennis shoes, the smashed pieces
of a Seagram's bottle, textbooks . . .

Kneeling to work in the diesel wind
I'm swept by cloud shadows
gliding like huge weightless buses

over the thruway. Young guys
in vans honk as they pass, or give the finger
for slowing them down. What drove me

at eighteen, or twenty-six,
what I wouldn't have done, I don't exactly
remember. I remember only the day

started as clouds began to climb
on each other's backs, then piled on
like the layers of our sleep, a sleep more

comforting, harder to leave
each morning. I remember the taste
of an orange eaten alone in the kitchen;

how you turned and reached
when I left the bed; the small assurances
we exchange before separate days.

I wipe my hands on dry grass, lock the tire
in with the sneakers and the evidence
of blown time, punch the radio on.

And I see the clouds that are bending
across my windshield as I ease
into the nervous stream.

Dragonfly Dance

for Philip Levine

He lights on the wooden handle
of the wheelbarrow, steady as a thumbtack.
Sleek models for the artificial
ball and socket, gold limned eyes swing up

at me, fix my image. Imagine—
two tiers of transparent wings
and a paper-weight body, pale violet,
clipping the air around the garden!

Once he sees my moving height
the living threads shoot between us;
he jerks up like a blown leaf
and does an airy dance, a minuet

around my body. We don't touch,
only measure each other in the sunny quiet,
labor to see into a different form
we might have taken. Then he flys off.

I should be that thin, I think,
and walk inside, where the white paper waits
and the people I am asked to carry,
who must also carry me.

Melinda

Daughter of a friend, I know they're thinking
as we walk to the mini-park by the Sound, you
bouncing between the cracks and singing
for no one. Of course they're right—my blue
eyes against your deep browns, your little storm
of Italian curls beside my mild English waves
disclaim me from any title beyond uncle. But
for now your shiny heart belongs to no one,
like your songs, like all those things you see
in the sky outside your window at night
when you should be sleeping. I could tell you
there is time to learn such tricks of speech
as *possession*, and worse, to be damaged
so many ways by words; then cultivate red
nails and quick tears, claw your way out. . . .
But you'd just be scared, and I would be
wrong. Now you dance in the kitchen and think
it's the roof, you make up jokes on the spot,
you whistle two blocks to a friend you can't see
and the friend comes running; you sing me
to the park. There I watch you shoot down
the slide, and I'm glad there's no way
I can harm the woman I know waits inside you,
since we have no future. "Now this!" you cry,
and I swing you on the fenceless gate
with its circle of dust for small feet to drag
and you yell "Faster, faster!" your eyes locked
    wide and your hair
flailing at my face as you whirl past.

Trevor and the Swarm of Gnats

Naked to the waist,
he rides tear-ass around the umbrella
until even near collisions
begin to bore him, and he abandons
Big Wheel on Daddy's porch,
where it lies, a huge blue rabbit.
He hesitates on the step, then plunges
into a lawn steaming with noon sun
and wanders from Frisbee
to chrysanthemum,
throwing, or crushing
as each object suggests
until he comes to the meeting
of forest and grass, and gazes in.

It's then the nervous
cloud of gnats drifts out of trees
and settles over his head.
He is touched, his eyes drawn
from shaded moss and fern
to center in the swarm, his face
filled with the astronomer's
pale wonder. This is first ecstasy,
and even as mother calls through
the kitchen window, bending his name
across the air, his eyes are held by the swirl.

Unafraid of transformations, he slowly dips
his hand inside the living galaxy
and holds it there, quiet as the sun.

A Dream Shared in
the Country

At first pale yellow tattoos the leaves,
a page of newsprint joins a spiral
of dust whirling through the parking lot;
the moon itself falls behind an Antique Shop,

the one with blue depression glass
in the window. But we don't understand
these tics of memory, fragments curving back
with the parabolic strength of family snapshots

and, one too many, causing panic: "Christ,
my face—is that really what I looked like?"
No answer. She puts her hands back under the lush
black quilt, as if it were a contract,

an agreement with the god of sleep
that her dream follow a strict plot line.
"Darling," she says to my back, "I'm freezing
to death, please shut the window." I do.

But somehow it's not obvious which illusions
we have in common. *There's a star*,
she says, for example, and points to a star,
faint, tucked into folds of gray cloud,

a star . . . and yes, she thinks, we'll wind down
like that, how lovely! —In the slow death
of burning without feeling
heat, being the essential heart of fire itself . . .

After this last part she moans,
her eyes close and the whole length of our bodies
finds meeting, adheres. I stare unconsciously
through the barn window at the receding

treetops and imagine us floating there
rinsed by the airy euphoria;
watching our lives from the height of street lamps,
red scratches along our shoulders and hips . . .

I grope for her hand in the soup of leaves.
Under the wind's harsh calculus, the lullaby —
pure, attentive song we sing to get back
time the earth peels away, in its turning.

Conception in Venice

We expected pale colors and foul water,
a crush of Germans in the lace
and glass shops, the pocked-stone
imp, the nude and the twisted beggar
haunting the garden on Torcello.
And we'd heard of the nightly
transformation: dusky romance sweeping the Piazza
San Marco, the corny music that lifts pigeons
and wakes the sleeping Doge, causing
his fabulous jewels to rise
to the canal's surface, and dance.
The first night in we blew a hundred-
sixty, American, to glide the city's mossy veins,
good cheap wine on the velvet seat
between us, the gondolier
pointing out the palace of Casanova
in broken English, and shouting what sounded
like *Hui!* when we came to blind turnings.
But there was not one painting, not one gilt horse
unsurrounded by squads of Italian school kids
and we gave up history for seafood,
for long afternoons in the hotel
trying out new love in a liquid tongue.
It worked. This is for you, child,
now swelling the veins in Sarah's belly,
words to mark the time and place you chose
to return to earth, unexpected,
Pisces rising from pale green waters.

Rolling in Clover

for Laura

My daughter practicing her vowels at dawn
woke us happy. All week the sky pressed—
humidity 95. Today the sun is pure, held
by the light air gently, breatheable.

Poplars throw small change in the wind.
Milkweed spore fly past my blanket,
delicate aliens looking for the new world.
A kingfisher pauses, pinned to a cloud

like a furious thought, seconds before
the kill. . . . This horizon's a cup of leaves
I try to fill with vision, though the trees
are enough, and the clouds revolving

as on a sphere of glass. *Description's
a way in, that place where things come back
to themselves,* I write, then hold the page
up for the wind to erase. Oh, any weather

can heal, but if the scene's too pretty
to write, and you are suddenly as happy
as you'll ever be, get down in the clover,
father, down in the green sunlight, and roll.

On the Failure of
All Love Poems

I think if love has any use for words
the contact's vague: fog touching the surface
of a lake, a blind man entering an unfamiliar room.
And if you dare to bring up the moon, taped
and retaped like a poor kid's baseball
righteous groans begin to rise from the orchestra
(though they may be crying in the cheap seats)—
everyone knows the moon is all thumbs,
a place human shadows crumple into silt
instantly. What else then? The flowers,
of course the flowers and of course the music
of weekends, the reggae, the Ella, the Bach,
and the side trip to Champlain, which I thought
was ocean; the music of all huge waters.
Lunching on the pier, the paper blew from your
sandwich across the thin beach. When I
brought it back you said *love* again—
it was when we'd just started saying it.
What else then? The silent return to the
hotel, our bodies moving easy as planet
and moon, until I pointed to a tiny blue
flower growing from a sidewalk crack
and asked you, the botany major, its name.
I remember you laughed, and said it wasn't
your specialty—it was cultivated, and must
have gotten free somehow to have ended here,
wild and frail. You laughed, and didn't know.

Song for Prophecy in a
Rainy Season

Kneeling on a flat stone, I notice the waterbug's
feet cast round shadows on the sandy bed,
four points revolving like a dream of molecules.
Skunk cabbage, guardians of the brook,
clustered imps with their palms held out
offer bitter warning to deer, coon, the night

drinkers. Cold infusions fed this brook—
three weeks of rain. I stand listening
to its silky engine. What secrets the wildflowers
tell! I would blush if I knew their names.
The sun leaps in the wrinkles of the water's face,
papery leaves of the silver elm

scallop down, held tight all winter.
Oh, I am a little younger than the atom gone crazy
and have entered my thirties wondering
at the height and blankness of certain walls;
soft explosion of crocus and daffodil, love for one
woman, breeze from the Atlantic, promising,

promising . . . Now, caught in the first real sun
for months: a cock pheasant, insane,
screaming from the brush of the far bank!
No. We have wasted our time in the elements.
Someone else must find a way into the arrowed buds
and emerge, speaking in a voice washed by green light.

About the Author

Jeffrey Skinner has worked in a variety of fields, and is now both poet and private investigator. He lives with his wife and young daughter in Stamford, Connecticut where he is vice president and general manager of Gleason Plant Security. Skinner was educated at Rollins College (B.A., 1971) and at Columbia University (M.F.A., 1978). *Late Stars* is his first book.

About the Book

This book has been composed in Bembo by Marathon Typography Service, Inc., of Durham, North Carolina. It is printed on 60 pound Warren's Old Style by Thomson-Shore, Inc. of Dexter, Michigan.